Rock Dreams

Guy Peellaert – Nik Cohn

Rock Dreams

POPULAR LIBRARY • NEW YORK

Illustrations copyright © 1973 by Guy Peellaert. Text copyright © 1973 by Nik Cohn.

Published by arrangement with AMACO ESTABLISHED

Permissions

"Guitar Man"—Elvis Presley (RCA)
"Brenda Lee"—Chuck Berry (Chess)
"Every Night (I Pray)"—The Chantels (End)
"Claudette"—The Everly Brothers (Cadence)
"He's a Rebel"—The Crystals (Philles)
"Sally Go Round the Roses"—The Jaynettes (Long Nite)
"Be True to Your School"—The Beach Boys (Capitol)
"Strawberry Fields"—The Beatles (Parlophone)
"Having a Party"—Sam Cooke, (RCA)
"New York Mining Disaster"—The Bee Gees (Polydor)
"I'm a Lonesome Fugitive"—Merle Haggard (Capitol)
"My Generation"—The Who (Track)

Acknowledgments. We would like to thank Karel Anthierens, **Dupuis;** Jacques Barsamian, Michael Choquette, **Rolling Stone;** C.B.S., Phillippe Selz, Cinema International; Jan Donkers, Bernard Eisenschitz, Paul Gillon, **Hara Kiri,** Pierre Herman, Warner Columbia Films; Jean-Pierre Lavigne, Frank Lipsik, Jean Mareska, Kiney-Filipacchi; Marjolijn, **Aloha; Melody Maker;** Phillippe Paringaux, **Rock and Folk;** Gilles Petard, Pathé Marconi; Bob Powel, **Country Music People Magazine;** Peter Schröder, Michael Taittinger, Jean-Pierre Tuil, Ruud Van Dulkenraad, **Muziek Express.** Our particular thanks and appreciation are extended to Ann Herouet, Béatrice Babinet, Barbara Bijl, Anne-Marie Corlin, Jessa Darieux, Gil de Grandsaigne, Marie Donon, Françoise Guillot, Michel Smet, Emilie Van Hees, Grietje Van Heijningen, Roger Wolfs, Studio Photon S.A.; their willing assistance has often given us much needed encouragement.

POPULAR LIBRARY • NEW YORK

For Alberta

"Under The Boardwalk"

. . . was a record by the Drifters early in the sixties, later revived by the Rolling Stones: a marvelous song about privacy and escape.

It is set on an American beach, in high summer, with everything heat and noise and bustle. A world full of blaring music, and over-filled bikinis, and hamburger stalls. Smells of greasy french fries, sounds of the amusement park. Everybody staring. No secrecy and no chance of ease. But under the boardwalk it feels different. Under the boardwalk you are hidden away, where no heat can reach you, nor any hassles. Lying on a blanket with your girl, and the radio soft beside you, and a bottle of Coca Cola, ice-cold. The beach is only a few feet away, yet infinitely distant, as though only dreamed, in flashes. An inferno—sweat, din, exposure —but here you lie in shade and are inviolate. Nothing can reach you, nobody can touch you. All you do is daydream. These daydreams, more than anything, are what this book is about. Rock as a secret society, as an enclosed teen fantasy. Other volumes, dozens of them, have dealt with it in much more solemn terms, as sociology or theology, mysticism, subculture or art. "Rock Dreams" deals in images and obsession: Rock 'n' Roll romances.

We have tried, above all, to catch the most crucial dreams in each new stage as Rock has developed. To convey the different flavors of different phases, how they felt and what were those visions: the ways in which those visions changed, grew up more complex, diversified, and the ways in which they remained always the same. Rock in its myths, its heroisms and villainies; its triumphs and catastrophies; in its landscapes, props and backdrops; its ironies, its cruelties and sentimentalities, its celebrations, its fetishes. Its ever-changing, never-changing rituals.

Roots

Rock, in the beginning, sprang from everywhere — Rhythm 'n' Blues and Country, romantic white balladeering and Hollywood musicals, novelties, electronic gimmickry, barbershop quartets and just plain dance music. Previously each had formed a separate stream; Rock 'n' Roll snatched them up and flung them together wholesale, in every kind of bizarre and anarchic marriage. For a time there was utter chaos. Then came Elvis and, with him, a whole new order.

FRANKIE GOES HOLLYWOOD

Bobby-sox brigades cause near-riot scene

Sinatra needed a cordon of guards to get by his fans at Grand Central

Frankie Laine. "I believe, for every drop of rain that falls, a dollar grows..."

Left to right: Teresa Brewer, Perry Como, Tennessee Ernie Ford, Danny Kaye, Judy Garland, Guy Mitchell, Doris Day, Tweety Pie, Frankie Laine, Jo Stafford, Bing Crosby, Dean Martin, Gene Kelly, Louis Armstrong, Rosemary Clooney, Howard Keel.

Johnnie Ray.
Million-dollar Teardrop,
Nabob of Sob,
The Little White Cloud That Cried.

Joe Turner.

From Kansas City, at two forty pounds, Big Joe
can drink both bourbon and beer;
can tear down walls with his bare hands,
can chew pig-iron and spit it out as razor blades,

can kill a man with a smile;
can holler like a mountain-jack,
can swallow hogsbacks whole, and
make love all night long;
can do whatever you can do – Big Joe can do it better.

Hank Williams. Within Hank Williams, two beings coexisted, intertwined but incompatable. The first wore rodeo spangles, picked guitars and yodelled, in the classic image of the Country'n'Western cowpoke; the second was Southern white trash – depression-raised and underfed, restless, insecure, eternally mistrustful. As one, Hank became the greatest star of the Grand Ole Opry, unchallenged King of Country; but as the other, he lived on highways and in motels and cafeterias, got drunk, wrecked his marriage, never stopped travelling and very soon died, of heart failure and too many pills, in the back of an automobile.

Elvis Presley. Outside the poolhall, standing in the sun, I was minding my business and combing my hair, when along came a carhop and called me dirty names.
First the length of my hair, then the cut of my clothes, and then the way that I curled my lip – he stared into my eyes, and spat on my blue suede shoes.
Right there on the pavement, with one foot in the gutter, I cut him all to pieces.

You saw me crying in the chapel – the tears I shed were tears of joy. I made a hundred million dollars, sold a hundred million records, broke a hundred million hearts; dreamed a hundred million dreams.
America made me and, on my knees, I offered up thanks.

Now, when I come home, late at night, my slippers are waiting in front of the fire, my pipe is on the mantleshelf, and Priscilla is sitting up in bed, with curlers in her hair. Then I kiss her on either cheek, and on her lips like cherries, and I hold her close to my heart. "Welcome home", she says, and at last I am at peace.

"Elvis Presley is the King.
Left to right: Vince Taylor, Tommy Steele, P.J.Proby, Billy Fury, Tommy Sands, Rick Nelson,

We were at his crowning ..."
Elvis Presley, Tom Jones, Eddie Cochran, Terry Dene, Ritchie Valens, Fabian, Cliff Richard.

Good Hard Rock. Barbarians at the gates: into the breach created by Haley and Presley there surged battalions of converts. Wild men with uncombed hair, fluorescent suits and voices like power drills, who jumped on pianos or did the splits, grovelled on their knees, shook their hips or hollered themselves into states of bug-eyed trance. Last-ditch desperadoes, emerging from swamps and backwoods to blow up everything that Tin Pan Alley had held most sacred – decorum, good taste, true romance. They sweated, roared and swaggered to the limit; tore the temple down, and razed it to the ground.

Bill Haley. People ask me, Bill, how can you do this?
You a musician, a grown man and a pro, how can you play this trash?
This jungle music?
Listen, I tell them, don't knock it.
I mean, I'm thirty years old, and I have a wife and five children to support, and I scuffled ten years for a break, and now I finally got it, and I'm not about to let it go, not for anyone, no matter what.
So I grin, and I keep on grinning, and I don't stop grinning until they turn the lights out.
Listen, I say, it's a living.

Fats Domino. At three hundred pounds, Fat Daddy was not all flab: each night, in trial of strength and stamina, he would shove his grand piano clean across the stage, bumping it with his thigh. "Clean living keeps me in shape," he said. "Righteous thoughts are my secret, and New Orleans home cooking."

Little Richard. Who raised the dead? Who caused the blind to see, the crippled to walk, the afflicted to take their ease? Who raised his hand and the sinners were saved? Who roared like a lion, cooed like a dove? Who howled like a coyote, yammered like a jackal? Who crept like a crawling king-snake? Who prayed, who wept? Who got down on his knees? Who flew like a swallow, a bat, an albatross? Who was clean? Who was dirty? Who broke down the door? Who jumped in the fire?

Little Richard
Penniman,
Ooohh, my soul,
That's who!

Bo Diddley. Here rode Bo Diddley, gunslinger and mean roadrunner, with his two feared accomplices, Jerome and the Duchess. Right across America, these three were known as desperadeos beyond equal and, whenever they hit town, the competition scattered.

"I am the biggest, the baddest, the fastest in the land," cried Bo and, to be sure, he almost was.

Jerry Lee Lewis. "Either be hot or be cold. If you are lukewarm, the Lord will spew you forth from his mouth". Thus spoke Jerry Lee and he rampaged through the land, with his piano, his bible and his thirteen year old wife. Night after night, leaping high upon the piano, he preached with fiery tongues, in sermons of arrogance and lust. Then his audience would surge forward and storm the stage, like converts, to shake his hand and be blessed.

Gene Vincent. After he hurt his leg, Gene Vincent always performed in pain and the possibility of collapse, and he stood on stage without moving, leaning forward, with his bad leg half-bent in front of him.

Eddie Cochran. Summertime blues: Betty Lou left for camp, Dad won't let me have the car, I got canned from the gas station, my suede shoes got oil on them, I have a dollar eighty two in the back pocket of my jeans. Tonight I came down on Main Street, with nothing to do and nowhere to go, and I bought myself a coke. For three hours, I sat there thinking, sipping, watching the girls go by. But all I could do was watch.

Chuck Berry. Once upon a time Chuck was Charles, just another flash dude in a barbershop. A brown-eyed handsome man, it's true, but all his sass had no direction and he felt trapped. Then one day, while he was sweeping up some loose clippings, he slipped and almost took a tumble. Instead of falling flat on his face, however, he did the

nat changed everything. In an instant, he was transformed into a superman. They called him the St. Louis Tiger and he was
. poet, a lover, a necromancer
"his man and his Duck Walk," said Alan Freed, "are destined to make history..."

Buddy Holly. Hey, what happened? One moment I was in Lubbock, Texas, and I had bad teeth, bad eyes and sang with my nostrils and adenoids, hiccoughing and whining. Everyone said I was crazy, so I left and came to New York, an I met a man who straightened me teeth, gave me new glasses, dressed me up real Italian sharp.
Next he called me Buddy Holly, and what kind of name is that? Then he sent me out on tour, and put me on TV, and now I'm a Rock 'n' Roll star.
I like it. Everywhere I go, girls scream at me, boys ask for my autograph and I ride around in a Cadillac. But sometimes I can't believe it – I remember Lubbock, Texas, and everybody laughing and I ask myself, can it last?

Duane Eddy.

Have Twang Will Travel.

"I quit my job down at the car lot,
Left my mamma a goodby note,
By sundown I'd left Kingston
With my guitar under my coat.
I hitched all the way down to Memphis,
Put up at the Y.M.C.A. –

For the next few weeks I kept haunting
  the bars,
Just lookin' for a place to play.
Well, I thought my pickin' would set
  'em on fire,
But nobody wanted to hire
A guitar man.
So I slept in the hobo jungle,

I roamed a thousand miles of track
Till I found myself in Mobile, Alabama,
At a club they called Big Jack's.
A little four-piece group was jammin',
So I took my guitar and I sat in,
And showed 'em what the band would
  sound like
With a swingin' little guitar man..."

The Everly Brothers. Such nice boys, those Everlys, with their hair swept back so neat and their manners so unassuming. But then they played their guitars, their voices slept like salmon and their heads drew very close together, until their lips were almost touching. Then they looked lost and most beautiful, like lovers or deadly enemies.

Highschool. Out in the jungles, wild Rockers sweated, screeched and stampeded; but in Highschool, meanwhile, everyone was cute and clean, perfectly behaved. From each year's class, the most promising pupils would be selected to come to Philadelphia, for special tuition on Dick Clark's American Bandstand, where diplomas were automatic passports to glamour, fame and wealth. With such high rewards, the competition for places was fierce and, for each successful applicant, there was different role to play, a different saga...

Left To Right Standing: The Fleetwoods: Barbara Ellis, Gary Troxel, Gretchen Christopher. Connie Francis. Dick Clark. Brenda Lee. The Teddy Bears: Annette Bard, Marshall Leib, Phil Spector. **In The Rear:** Buddy Knox.
Sitting: Frankie Lymon, Pat Boone, Paul Anka, Frankie Avalon, Ricky Nelson, Fabian, Tommy Sands.

OVERWEIGHT ? OUT OF SHAPE ? A FAILURE WITH THE GIRLS ?

Let Paul Anka tell how you too can be a man ...

GUYS,
BE LIKE PAUL ANKA,
TURN FATNESS INTO FITNESS.

Brenda Lee

"Brenda Lee, she's a sophomore,
Studied as the years went by,
She didn't dance, didn't date –
Always had an alibi.
But she shook up everybody
At the prom dance at Central High."

Fabian. But not all time was fun and games. Even in Highschool, hearts could be broken, and young dreams shattered, and many rings that were given in love were returned in spite and bitter tears.

"Every night, I go to bed,
Fall on my knees and I pray,
For my love.

Although he doesn't love me,
Keep him safe, just for me,
I pray."

Frankie Avalon and Annette Funicello. Weekends we go to the beach and have a barbecue, or surf, or just sit in the sand, holding hands. After dark, we break out some cokes and dance to the transistor radio, or smooch along to the Platters, with all their beautiful melodies, like "Only You" and "Twilight Time".

hen Annette snuggles up and whispers in my ear, runs her fingers through my hair. The moon shines on the water and the aves are breaking at our feet, while I take her in my arms, and she puckers up for a long, lingering kiss.
Gee, can't wait till we get married...

Phil Spector. Phil came to class with problems. He'd grown up in the Bronx and his father was dead and, to be perfectly honest, he had picked up some quite unappetising habits. Also, he was undersized and Jewish and spoke in a funny squeaky voice. Although he showed undoubted promise, he never really fitted in and, when he dropped out of class, after only one semester, the rest of the kids were secretly relieved.

Pat Boone and Connie Francis. Of all past graduates, the school was most proud, and justly so, of these. Mr. Boone had grown into a fine and upstanding young father of six, whose strong sense of morality was combined with an open, cheerful winsomeness; while curvacious Miss Francis, a bouncy bundle of fun, was accomplished in several languages – a rare blend of brains and beauty. Without question, they were both fine models for all young Americans to follow.

Class Disbands. Sad to say, all good things must come to an end and, after 1960, hit by changing fashions, Highschool was forced to limit its activities and, finally, to shut down altogether.

Luckily, their training had equipped many graduates to launch new careers in other fields, such as films, cabaret and business, while Dick Clark himself continued to thrive as before. From time to time, he even held class reunions, occasions for reminiscence and the greatest jocularity.

But a few alumni proved less fortunate. Among the features of the school had been its tolerance and universal good-will, and the way in which it welcomed all applicants alike, even those from the less privileged sections of the community. Naturally enough, however, such cases paid higher fees on entry, and were rewarded with lower grades of a diploma, so that, when school was finished, many of them foundered.

One example was Frankie Lymon. Originally among the youngest, most talented and most personable of all students, Frankie slowly drifted into obscurity and degradation. In the end, aged almost thirty, he was found dead of a drug overdose.

Land Of A Thousand Dances. For a moment, after the first fury of Rock'n'Roll, and the idyll of Highschool, there was a lull, as though the storm might have blown itself out. Early in the sixties, there were no great myths, and no millenia. Just a few isolated arrivals, a scattering.

But then came Chubby Checker, fat boy from the slaughterhouse. Immediately energy and speed returned, to be expressed in a land of a thousand dances. Soon the Twist was joined by the Madison, which gave way to the Locomotion, which was followed in turn by the Jerk, and then there was the Shake, and the Wa-Watusi, the Mashed Potato and the Climb, the Swim and the Duck, the Monkey and the Pony, the Fly, the Skate and the Boogaloo, the Harlem Shuffle, the Philly Dog and more, many more.

Performers hardly mattered in this – what counted were the songs and, most of all, the beats. Rock was never so mindless, so uncomplicated and never more fun. In this same period, also, there dawned the golden age of the Teendream. In New York and Philadelphia, and on the West Coast, songwriters formed themselves into teams – Goffin/King, Shuman/Pomus, Mann/Weil and more – and methodically, almost mechanically, began to pour forth an unending succession of ballads: True Teen Romances, yearning and aching, computerised, corny and most marvellous.

Roy Orbison.
"I'm going to be so happy for the rest of my life,
When my brand new baby is my brand new wife,
Claudette…"

Claudette was a song that Roy Orbison wrote for the Everlys;
she was also his wife. Together, they rode their motorbikes on
the highways every day, for year after year. Then one day
Claudette crashed. After that, Roy rode alone.

Del Shannon. Stranger in town – Del Shannon may have sounded and looked like a lumberjack but he cracked just like a soda-jerk. He was incessantly on the run, broke and alone, and his true loves all betrayed him.
In the naked city, there was an eternal thunderstorm and the raindrops mingled with his tears.

The Drifters. Under The Boardwalk ... and On The Roof...
or cruising down Broadway, or lounging in the balcony at Saturday night movies, or shaking it down at the neighbourhood dance
the Drifters were masters of escape. Over ten years, they changed everything about themselves, their personnel and songwriters

audience and style, but their basic message was always the same: Somewhere in this city, so vast and impersonal, so loud and harsh and filthy, there is still a refuge, where nothing can reach you, where fun is still fun. That's where we go to hide, out of the holocaust, and hurry, we've saved the last place for you.

Phil Spector. Strange resurrection of Baby Phil, the Highschool drop-out: arriving in New York, he slept in offices, on floors and benches and desk tops, until finally he was let loose to produce a record. Then, at a single shot, he paid back twenty years' accumulation of rage. Out pured wildest torrents of pent-up energy, invention, insanity, malice, fantasy, grotesquerie and when the smoke cleared, he stood revealed in Hollywood technorama: a colossus: true inheritor of Cecil B. de Mille: ultimate Rock'n'Roll showman, teendreamer and bullshitter, genius and freak.

ms

He's A Rebel....
"...Just because he doesn't do
What everybody else does,
That's no reason why
We can't share a love."

"Leader Of the Pack". Disaster, destruction, doom: of all Teendreams, the Shangri-Las created the most mythic, the most tragic, the most kitsch. Three schoolgirls in black leathers, they wailed like sirens, harbingers of trauma, and deaths were two a dime.

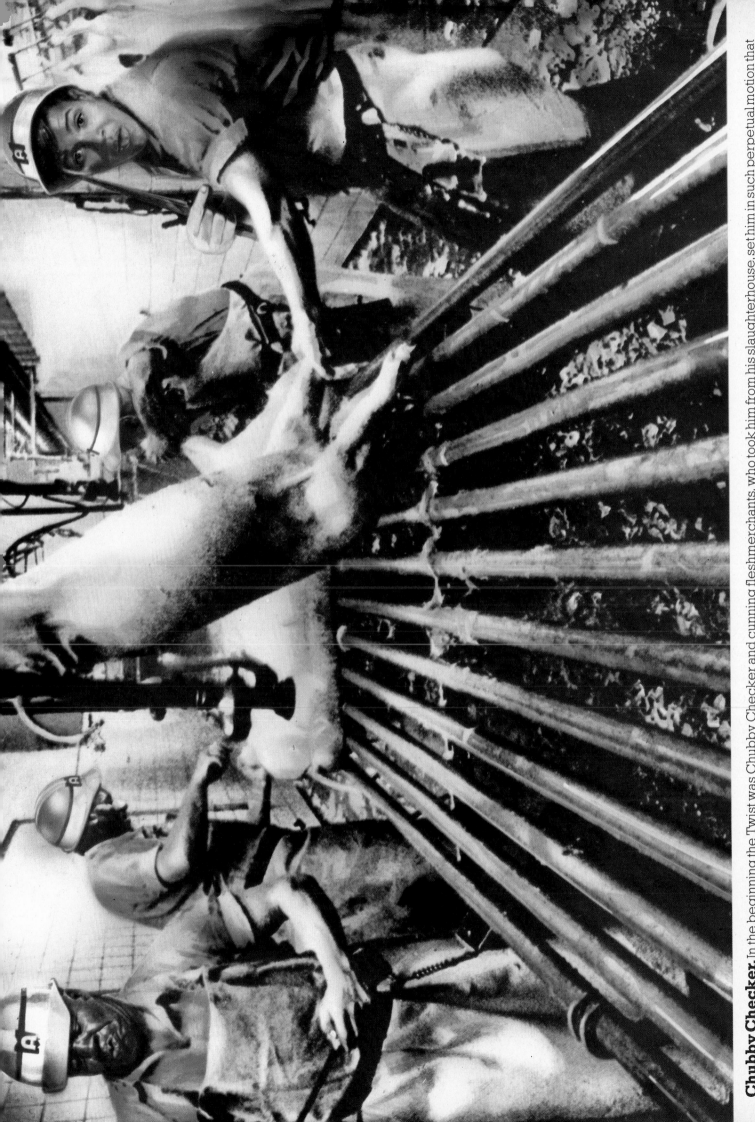

Chubby Checker. In the beginning the Twist was Chubby Checker and cunning fleshmerchants, who took him from his slaughterhouse, set him in such perpetual motion that he lost 40 pounds and unleashed him on the nation. They got rich, but he did not.

Twist. Thus far it was simple – Chubby demonstrated and teenagers followed his instructions. But then grown-ups began to latch on as well, which was most unexpected, and especially the rich, the fashionable and the internationally élite, which was even more so. For the first time, without warning, Rock 'n' Roll was chic, and the Peppermint Lounge overflowed with mandarins.

The Promised Land. California was teen heaven, perfection, where the sun was always shining, where the cosmic surfer's wave unfurled towards infinity, where everyone was golden, young and beautiful forever. For every girl, there were two boys, and

so they lounged by the poolside, drinking cold beers and counting the passing bikinis, or they played touch football, in eternal summer, or they drag-raced, made love at the drive-ins, watched technicolor sunsets, led plans, wrote songs...

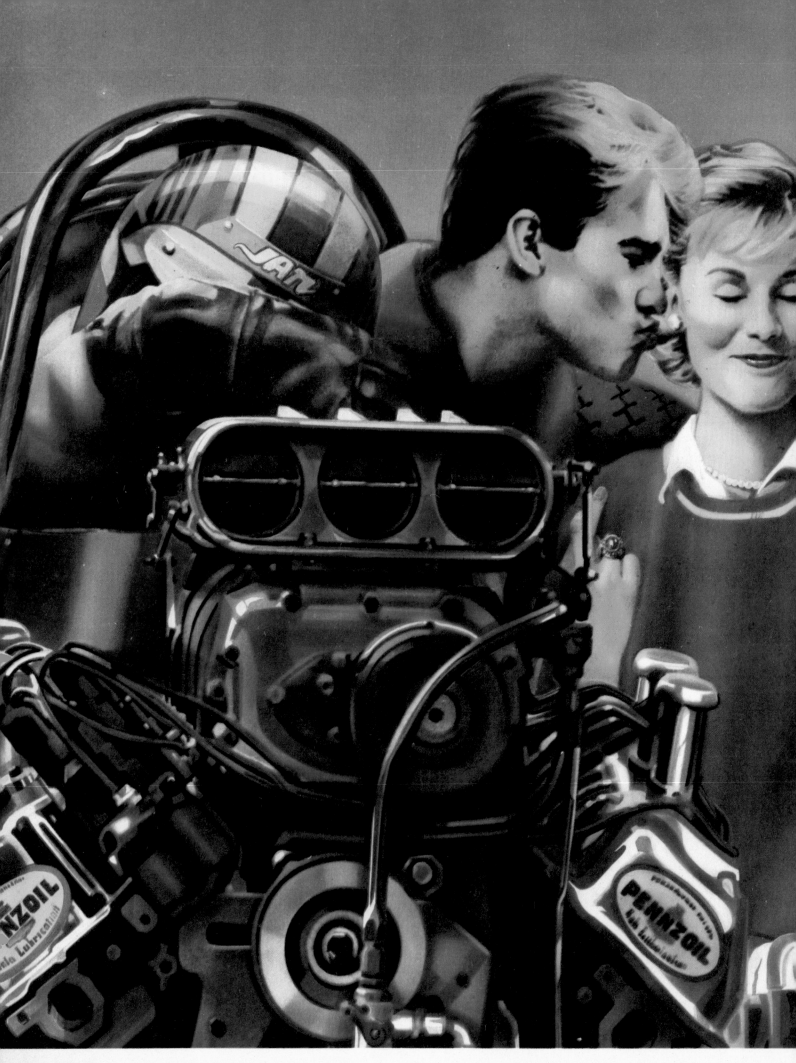

Jan & Dean. "Burn up that quarter mile...".

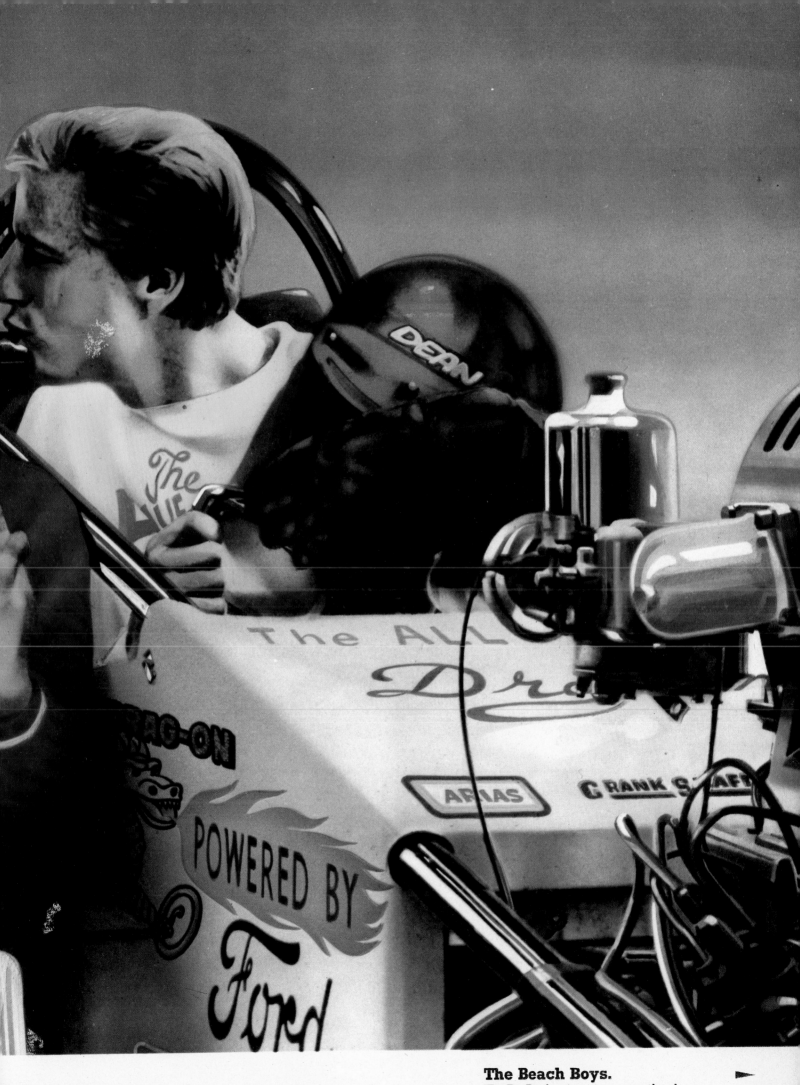

The Beach Boys.
"Ra Ra Ra, be true to your school,
Just like you would to your girl or guy…".

California Girls. "We've been having fun all summer long...".

Brian Wilson. Vacations, Carl worked at the gas station, for a dollar an hour, while Denny took the car...and Brian sat at home, in his room, with his weight problems and his ear disease, his allergies, his pathological shyness, and wrote dreams about outdoors, where the sun was always shining, where the cosmic surfer's wave unfurled towards infinity, and where everyone was golden, young and beautiful forever.

The Beatles. And then there were the Beatles and everything was different. They introduced reality, a certain worldliness and Teendreams were doomed. From now on, Rock's fantasies grew steadily more complex, more cerebral and self-conscious. Out of nowhere England became the fulcrum, London the rallying point and the great new dream was freedom – performers were no longer computerised, no longer the abject slaves of the industry. Hereafter they could jump off their conveyor belts and rush about frantically in search of honesty, meaning, truth. Celebration was intense.

ne take you down..."

"...'cos I'm going to..."

"...Strawberry Fields".

"Nothing is real...".

"...and there's nothing to get hung about".

"Strawberry Fields Forever".

Cilla Black. Once the Beatles had made Liverpool famous, Brian Epstein and other managers kept returning and, between them, they signed up every singer and group they could find. By the time they were through, it seemed that hardly anyone, able-bodied and under-thirty, had been left behind.

P.J. Proby. "I don't do", said Proby. "Maestro, I am".

The Who. Week of 22-29 November, 1964

Credits

Monday	The Social Club, Goldhawk Road	£ 9
Tuesday	The Marquee	£ 10
Thursday	The California Ballroom, Dunstable	£ 12
Saturday	The Railway Arms, Neasden	£ 6
Record Royalties		N
TV and Radio fees		N
Total		**£ 3**

Debits		
replacement of guitars, drum kits, microphones, etc.	£	785
new clothes (Pete)	£	300
publicity	£	460
repairs to Roger's new car	£	80
Scotch of St. James, discotheques (Keith's account)	£	320
John's expenses (Luncheon Vouchers)	£	1.17.6
Total	**£ 1946.17.6**	

Loss on Week   £ 1576.17.6

The Adlib. The Adlib was a London discotheque, suspended high above the city, and there the Beatles held court, while all t[...]
rest of Rock clustered round, like courtiers round royalty.

Left to right: Keith Richard, Anita Pallenberg, Brian Jones, George Harrison, Jeff Beck, an unknown beauty, Keith Relf of the Yardbirds, Patti Boyd, Scott Walker of The Walker Brothers, Mrs. and Mr. Ringo Starr, Alan Price, John Lennon, Eric Burdon, Keith Moon, Charlie Watts, Mick Jagger, Marianne Faithful, P.J.Proby, Sandie Shaw, Zoot Money, Georgie Fame, Paul McCartney.

Ray Davies, and the Kinks. "What are we living for? Two-room apartment, second floor."

The Rolling Stones. First there were six small boys, who built themselves a palace of perpetual pleasures and gave all their lives to games. Sometimes their games were nice but, mostly, their games were naughty, nasty or downright disrespectful and they pulled rude faces, stuck out their tongues or dressed themselves in the strangest, the most disturbing costumes.

Then there were five, because the sixth, who had first thought of this palace, had now quarrelled with the others and been cast out. Nonetheless, the round of treats continued undiminished and there were japes, pranks, much more fun for all.

Then they were four, because the fifth had grown exhausted and had moved off round the corner. Now the games grew more and more uproarious, more and more violent, so that the downstairs' neighbours banged on the ceiling with brooms, to ask for quiet and decency. But "Hey, you, get off of my cloud" – that was the funsters' only response, and the volume rose still higher.

Then there were three, because the fourth had also grown exhausted, and the complete gang only reassembled on certain special occasions, when they were tired of seclusion and decided to raid the public parks. Now, in the search for continuous novelty, their games were ever-changing: in turn they played at revolution, and they played at martyrdom, and they even played at sanctity. Sooner or later, however, all flavours bored them.

Then there were two, because the third had flown off through the window and disappeared into the skies, and they sat among the debris, sated, slightly ageing but not too jaded to pull the same rude faces, or to stick out their tongues once more, as they'd done in the days of their first youth.

Then there was only one, all alone.
Immured in his palace of mirrors, he never grew any older and, even though his stock of games had long since run out, he went right on playing them, over and over and over.

Robert Zimmerman, His Journeys And Adventures: Hobo Bob. Very young and frail, Bob left his home one day and set forth to seek his fortune, with his possessions knotted in a red-spotted handkerchief and his pussycat at his heels. Then he slept in logging camps, in ditches and swamps and mudflats, next to railroad tracks and inside county jails, with only his guitar to keep him company, and he journeyed all through America.

New York Bob. Itinerant minstrel, he sang and played as he travelled and, somewhere on the road, his eyes opened wide and his soul was filled with purpose, a spirit of crusade. From that moment forward, his path was set and he bent himself to the ceaseless combatting of tyrannies, the righting of wrongs and overthrow of hypocrisies, until peace and love should spread through all

mankind. Thus, when at last he reached New York, he did not hesitate but rushed pellmell to Bleeker Street, where his message might best be understood. In bars and dimlit cellars, he sang through his nose and preached, and all who heard him were thunderstruck. **Left to right:** Phil Ochs, Bob Dylan, Judy Collins, Joan Baez, Allen Ginsberg

Superstar Bob. Soon his fame spread and he toured, grew rich and was worshipped. Messianic, he need only point his finger and the temples trembled before him. Now he travelled the world, a potentate, whose person was sacred, whose every word was scripture, and the multitudes flocked to see him. and touch him, and bend to kiss his feet.

But these things were not possible, for Zimmerman was no longer reachable. Brooding in grand hotels and limousines, he sat in judgment, or presented parables, but lived behind bullet-proof glass.

Country Bob. However, even Messiahs must have hobbies, and Zimmerman's was his motorbike, which proved to be his downfall. For one night, he fell off and broke his neck, and very nearly died. Thankfully, he was spared and, in time, he made his recovery. But, in the meantime, his tastes had changed, and age had made him mellow, so that he no longer played at potentates. Instead, he grew plump and became a Jewish patriarch, with six children and a homestead, where he sat at the kitchen table, where he sat at the kitchen table, with six children and a homestead, where he sat at the kitchen table, the American

Donovan: The Fool On The Hill

Simon & Garfunkel. Sounds of Silence, Scribbled On Subway Walls

Creeque Alley – The Mamas and the Papas. After Dylan, and after drugs, California was not the same. No more pleasures without thinking, no more pure circuits of sunshine, sand and surf. From now on the amusements were cerebral, usually inert – mornings in bed, afternoons on patios, evenings floating on magic cushions, on mountains or in canyons, with strange musics in the background.

The Beach Boys. But not for some. Drugged, bemused, prematurely middle-aged, the Beach Boys gazed out across the waves,

landscapes of their adolescence, and could never quite make up their minds, whether to stick with what they knew, or whether to head up into the canyons, float on those magic cushions...

The Byrds. The Byrds weren't so much a band as a focus, a training camp, where kids could come as novices and learn their trades and then depart, to become famous elsewhere, or disappear, or return, periodically, for a refresher course. Every year there was a new line-up, a different style.

Only Roger McGuinn remained constant, and the basic sound, and a sense of open spaces – mountains and blue skies, clean air.
Thus the Byrds came to represent release, dreamed-of freedom for all those white-fleshed groups, in Europe and the East and the
Mid-West, who sat cooped up in cities, slowly choking on diesel fumes.

The Lovin' Spoonful. For instance, the Spoonful: at first, in New York, they sat out on fire escapes, drank beers and enjoyed themselves as best they could. But as soon as they'd made some money, they changed their minds and headed out West instead, very fast, to join in the games.

Soul. From the moment that soul became Soul, around the mid-fifties, it was built on two central dreams: one black, one white. Black meant roots and was hard; white meant acquisition and was a great deal easier. Thus black might make you a God, but white made you safe.

The first was symbolised by ribs and grits, gospel, cheap sequinned glitter and plenty of funk, meaning sex; the second by Vegas and string sections, wigs, silk suits and all rough edges smoothed away. The crucial trick was balance – how to make the best of both.

A few, like James Brown, remained essentially black. Others, like Diana Ross and Ray Charles, plunged wholesale into whiteness. But the great majority tried for compromise, one foot in either camp.

So they talked and moved black. Their bankers, however, were white.

James Brown. Soul Brother Number One, with his private aeroplanes, in his silken robes, moving in a cloud of perfume and wealth; without rest, he travelled back and forth throughout his nation, like a sultan, like a healer, and everywhere that he moved, he dealt out largesse for the afflicted, joy for the sorrowing, rage for the faint at heart…

Ray Charles: The Fugitive's Dream.

Sam Cooke. Sam Cooke, shot dead in a motel, was black but ▶ dressed up white, sang Soul but wrote Teendreams, wagged his ass but gently, with a certain deference.

Otis Redding. Pity poor Otis, with his raggedy clothes and holes in his shoes – abused by his woman, scandalised and slandered, and riding out of town.
But, on stage, he always wore silks and smiled with the whitest teeth.

Smokey Robinson.
"There is a rose in Spanish Harlem,
A red rose up in Spanish Harlem."

Aretha Franklin. Sister Aretha, most righteous — so strong, so fierce, so domineering that she could cast aside her microphone and let fly unaided, to shatter plate-glass windows, topple skyscrappers, tear down whole cities, in the praise and service of her Lord.

Wilson Pickett and Solomon Burke. In the history of the universe, were ever hustlers to equal these? With their shades and rings and alligator shoes, and their creases as sharp as a knife, they had all the foxes running round in circles, all the dollar bills just dropping into their palms.

Tina Turner. Let's hear it for Mrs. Tina Turner, from Knoxville, Tennessee. Tina is a housewife by day, proud mother of four, and keeps busy with changing nappies, cleaning the apartment and cooking up her Southern specialities.
Mmmmmmm, when she gets to messing with those pots and pans, and out jumps the fried chicken, sweet potatoes, black-eyed peas and chitlins – husband Ike don't ever need to roam.

Finger lickin' good!
But Tina has another side. She has a secret ambition.
One day she wants to be a singer with the band and hit the road with a Big Roll show, entertaining the people wherever she goes, with savvy, class and Soul.

Stevie Wonder. A big hand for little Stevie, with magic in his fingertips and rhythm in his toes. Despite handicaps that would defeat most boys his age, he is not downhearted and goes right ahead, making his happy music, with that happy dancing beat, for all the happy people who flock to hear him.

The Supremes.

Joe Tex. And Brother Joe, most sneaky...
Who preached sermons of chastity, honour, humility, thrift? Who wagged his bony forefinger and sucked upon his lips, for the sins of all mankind? Then who made off with the collection, and seduced the Deacon's wife, in the name of Brotherly Love? Who else?

Chairmen Of The Board. After Jimi Hendrix, more black music sold in white markets; after the Beatles, more white sold in black. Out of that interaction, Soul developed a different approach – less stereotyped, altogether more personal. Nor was the change purely musical. Performers too grew idiosyncratic and self-willed. No more pre-packaging, no more funk by numbers –

the new wave created their own patterns and issued all their own orders. If there must be bullshit, at least they would manufacture their own.

Left to right: Isaac Hayes, Curtis Mayfield, Richie Havens, Roberta Flack, Sylvester Stewart, Taj Mahal, Marvin Gaye.

The Jackson Five. Just the same, old styles died slow. For every freak and rebel, there were still five nice boys in suits, who beamed and capered and made no fuss for anyone. Their clothes and hair might be altered, and some of the ways they talked but when you sliced them, they were big-eyed and cute, wholesome as Mom's apple pie.

Diana Ross. No cause for alarm: even now, after all these years, great ladies of the manor came back and cruised the streets, and gazed into tenements, and floated off down alleys, just to check that nothing had changed....

B.B.King. ...and it hadn't; not at absolute bedrock. At every other level, style and stance might change interminably. Right down at the bottom, however, the Blues remained...

Musicians. Inevitably, there came a point at which Rock had grown too complicated, much too various to be contained in a single direction, one overall fantasy, and it broke apart into different factions and schools. One group wished to be Musicians; another Bogeymen; yet another Poets. Or again, some aimed themselves at the future, some delved back to explore their own roots, some were content to celebrate the present. Rock 'n' Roll was played, and Jazz, and Country 'n' Western, traditional Folk and contemporary Folk, country Blues and urban Blues, pseudo-Classical, mock-Oriental and anything else that suggested itself. From now on, all was chaos; sometimes hopeless and sometimes splendid confusion.

In the past, music was not something that Rock had cared about but now it became most important. Earnest and concentrated as string quartets, groups would play for an hour without pausing, not to be mobbed or screamed at but in hopes of an ovation, rapturous 19th century Bravos and Huzzahs.   **Left to right:** Jeff Beck, Alvin Lee, Eric Clapton, Jimmy Page, Pete Townshend.

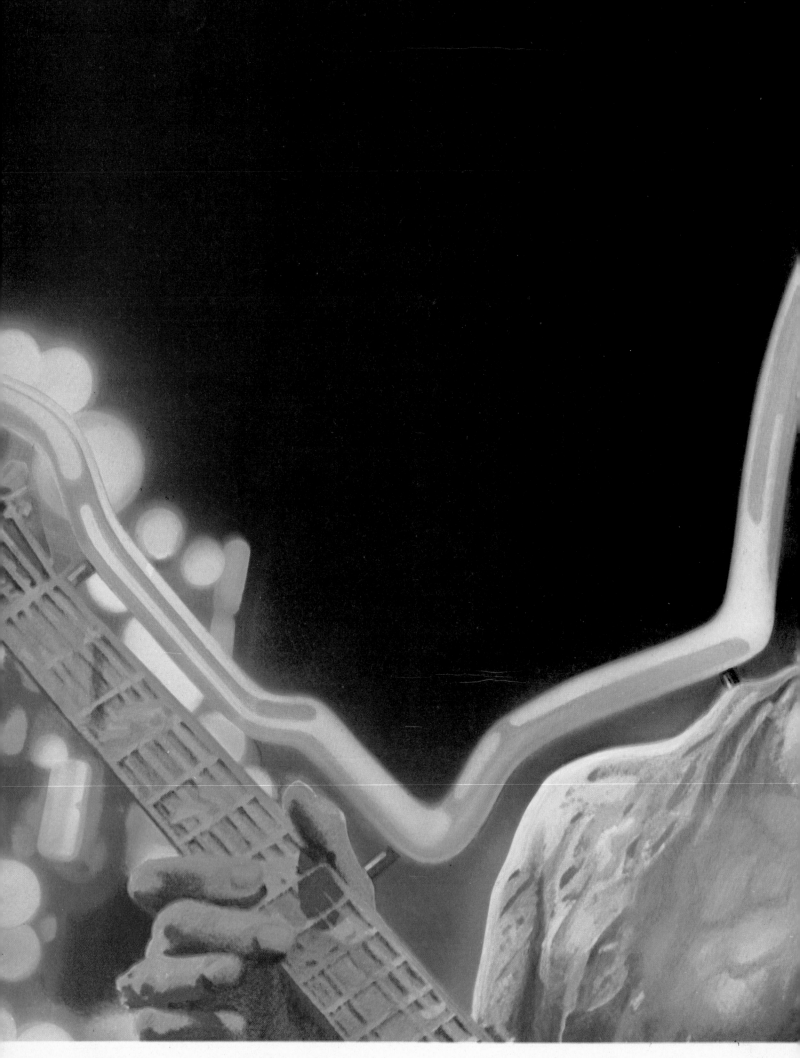

Jimi Hendrix. Backstage, Hendrix was leaning up against a fire hydrant between sets and listening to something infinitely far away, when a reporter approached him in a toupee and a plastic raincoat. "I'm from the New York Times," said the reporter and Hendrix, half-opening his eyes, smiled the very faintest and weariest of wry smiles. "Please to meet you," he said. "I'm from Mars."

Bogeymen. Evil had been.a cult in Rock ever since Screamin' Jay Hawkins in the mid-fifties but, after the Rolling Stones, it came into its flowering.

Every few months, one would turn to the TV and there would be a brand new villain, more anarchic, more satanic and more hideous than any of his predecessors.

Perversion, debauch and murder, rape and arson, deformity, criminal insanity and hopeless drug-addiction – all these became most fashionable matters to hint at, and therefore most profitable.

Arthur Brown. The God of Hellfire, apocalyptic, unspeakable, was nonetheless an Englishman. Hidden behind his robes and paint and voodoo masks, leaping and screaming, he laid waste the cosmos. But afterwards, drinking nice cups of tea and filling out the pools, he looked just like the lodger.

Ian Anderson (Jethro Tull). Troll, satyr, dirty old man: this was precisely the species of person that small girls are warned not to take sweets from. Appearing suddenly from behind park benches, or springing forth from the shrubbery, he would cock one leg in the air and totter round in small circles, half-hidden by hair.

Every so often, from somewhere within the tangle, an eye would stare out wildly and occasional hollers would be heard, or moans, or random cackles. Then, producing a flute from the depths of his dirty raincoat, he coaxed forth sound of the strangest sweetness and his victims could not help but follow wherever he led.

Alice Cooper. Outrageousness by numbers, shrewd and most calculating – it was as though Alice sat down with ready-reckoner to work out precisely what form of exhibitionism might be the naughtiest, dirtiest, most shocking, most titillating and most profitable at any given moment; then performed them ruthlessly, by stopwatch.

Joe Cocker and Leon Russell. "Punish me, oh master, for I have sinned." While Dracula slept, his servant strutted and cavorted and took the castle for his own, to bray like an ass, roar like a wounded bull. But then came dark and all was changed: the Count emerged from his slumbers, with eyes of flame, and Clovis went cringing, cowering back into his corner.

Doctor John the Night-Tripper: Walk On Gilded Splinters. Risen from swamps, cloaked in mists and mutterings, Doctor John had voodoo eyes that chilled the soul and spells of utmost potency. Bones rattled, cauldrons gurgled, lost souls groaned below – write him a bad review, and he might turn you into a toad.

On The Bus. After the age of Innocence, and the age of Inertia, there came an age of Extremities. During this phase, sparked by acid, the great trick was overstatement, to come on louder and weirder than all rivals; more freaked-out, more anarchic, more self-immolatory; more saintly and more satanic; more sexual, and more violent, and more militant; more profound; more original; more doomed. And yet, and yet...even here, in Edge City, the eternal California was not lost. Money was still made in large quantities, and mansions purchased, and the sunshine never flagged. Death and destruction roamed everywhere, yes, but always sugared by luxury.

The Jefferson Airplane, the Grateful Dead, Country Joe and the Fish. In San Francisco, Ken Kesey organised bus trips and tours, with excursions to many sites of local and national interest, and the rootless of the city hastened to clamber aboard, for whatever education they might derive.

Jim Morrison. At first Jim Morrison seemed no more than a marvellous boy in black leathers, made up by two queers on the phone. Later on, however, he emerged as something altogether more solemn. Not just a truck-stop rocker, nor even a golden stud, but a poet and a thinker, stuff full of profundities. Forthwith he embarked, like a Rock 'n' Roll Bix Beiderbecke, full speed ahead on the American route to romantic martyrdom.

Ruben and the Jets. Into the valley of death with Zappa: like horsemen of the apocalypse, the Mothers of Invention and GTOs and Wild Man Fischer, and the other acts in his three ring circus, roared on through the night, spreading plague and consternation wherever they passed.

Janis Joplin: "Gimme A Pigfoot And A Bottle Of Beer."

Country. Were fifties' dreams now extinct? Had the flowering of complexity and consciousness made all innocence redundant? Not entirely – to a large extent, the first myths survived in Country 'n' Western. The differences were immense, in roots, publics, age-groups, attitudes, but much of the flavour overlapped. In Country, as in nothing else, there were still true heroes and romances: the mystery, force and directness that Rock had once possessed but had long since lost.

Honky Tonk Angels. It wasn't God who made Honky Tonk Angels.

George Jones and Tammy Wynette. Stand by your man.

Dave Dudley. Truck Driving Man.
Six days on the road
And I'm gonna make it home tonight

Merle Haggard: I'm A Lonesome Fugitive.

"Down every road there's always one more city,
A fugitive must be a rolling stone.

I'd like to settle down but they won't let me –
I'm on the run, the highway is my home."

Jerry Lee Lewis: A Rocker Repents.

'What's Made Milwaukee Famous
(Made A Loser Out Of Me).''

Johnny Cash. Shot a man in Reno, just to watch him die.

The End. By and large Rock had grown self-important, predictable, flat. Much of the inner propulsion was gone, and so was the sense of kinship – the notion that performer and audience somehow formed a oneness. Its new images were mostly old images resurrected, only with added solemnity, and there was a jadedness, an exhaustion everywhere. "The day the music died", as Don McLean put it, and he was probably right. Rock had been a moment. The moment was past.

Real energy survived only in pockets, where scattered groups or individuals refused to be sucked under by the general smog and, steering clear of movements, fads, classifications, quietly went their own way. The Rock dreams that remained were bred in isolation: private visions, personal obsessions.

Velvet Underground. Shadow behind the shoulder; black slouch hat in a dark doorway; stilettos in the alley; a whimper by the window, and needles in the bathroom.

James Taylor.

"That's me up on the jukebox,
Singing that sad song"

Crosby, Stills, Nash and Young.

Highway songs, full of light and space.

Creedence Clearwater Revival. Back to the swamplands, where good hard Rock lived on, Saturday night dancehalls and back-seat love, french fries and cokes and ketchup, and fun was not yet forgotten...

The Who. From Shepherd's Bush Mods to time-machine mystic travellers, the Who embodied many different visions. But, finally, their fantasies paled before the fact, which was simply that they kept going out on the road, year after year, and played harder, longer and straighter for the people than anyone else.

The Band. The Band came from nowhere specific and their evocations were indistinct but they were the whole American past and all its space. Small towns in the civil war, at the turn of the century, during the Depression; saloons with cracked windows, and dance-halls with leaky ceilings, and hotel rooms with naked lightbulbs; highways, deserts, great rivers, mountains; girls glimpsed once or left behind or revisited many times, for a few nights' shelter; Saturday afternoon outings downstream or to the races, or over country roads in fourth-hand cars, with a bottle passed from hand to hand; truck stops, railroads, three-cell jails; gold rushes and oil strikes, eternal dreams of wealth; bad debts, hangovers; and movement, always movement – forever that sense of travelling back and forth across the land, trapped by its immensity and infinite change.

Lou Reed

David Bowie.

Rod Stewart. When it seemed that every singer must become a seer, every group a mystic sect, Rod Stewart came along and was simply a delinquent. In image, he wore steel-capped boots and rioted at football matches, tore up railway carriages, stuck out his tongue at the boss and left his best girl home on Saturday nights, while he went out on the beer with his mates. He left his flies undone, he was sick all over the carpet. No question, he was a very naughty boy.

Marc Bolan (T.-Rex)

"People try to put us down,
Just because we get around.
Things they do look awful cold..."

Sinatra: "...Hope I die before I get old."